Rune-Magic

Bibliotheca Runica

Number 1

Rune-Magic

Siegfried Adolf Kummer

Dedicated in Armanic Spirit
to all my loyal Runers

Translated and Edited

by Edred Thorsson

Yrmin-Drighten

The Rune Gild

First Edition, August 1993
First Printing, August 1993

Published by
Lodestar
P.O. Box 16
Bastrop, Texas 78602

runa@texas.net

Editor's Introduction

Siegfried Adolf Kummer was born in 1899 and was one of the pioneers of operative Runic studies in the early part of the 20th century. Little is known of his life or of his fate in the wake of the historical events of the Nazi era. He, along with Friedrich Bernhard Marby, was criticized by name in a report made to Heinrich Himmler by his chief esoteric runologist Karl Maria Wiligut. But what his fate was is unknown. At least one report has him fleeing Nazi Germany in exile to South America.

Kummer lived in and around Dresden in the years before the assumption of power by the National Socialists in 1933. He founded his Rune-School Runa in 1927. This presumably remained in operation until the National Socialist regime closed down all such organized activity soon after coming to power in 1933.

Runen-Magie was first published in 1933 as a part of the *Germanische Schriftenfolge* [Teutonic Writings Series]. It is to some extent a practical condensation of his larger work, *Heilige Runenmacht* published in 1932.

To understand Kummer's work completely, you will have to understand the magical world of Guido von List (1848-1919), the grandfather of the Germanic magical revival. The best introduction to List's ideas can be found in *The Secret of the Runes*, translated and introduced by Stephen E. Flowers in 1988. Also my *Rune Might* (Llewellyn, 1989) contains a historical and practical introduction to that world of Armanic rune magic generally pioneered by List.

Kummer's work largely belongs to that school of occult thinking prevalent in Germany during the first few decades of the 20th century which is sometimes called "Ariosophy" today. (This is a term coined by Lanz von Liebenfels based on analogy with the other "-sophies" of the day: Theosophy and Anthroposophy.) But more specifically Kummer identified himself as an **Armanist**, the school founded by Guido von List. Three of the most important general tenets of Armanism are: 1) All dualities, such as those between the body and the soul, or between humanity and nature, are both real at one level and only apparent at another. There is a singular essence, but it finds itself in differing conditions, which cause it to appear in various forms. But the **conditions** are in turn also real. This is the key to why techniques for the modification of physical conditions (eugenics, gymnastics, etc.) are seen in spiritual terms by Armanists.

2) All things in the cosmos are subject to a threefold cyclical process of Arising-Being-Passing away to new Arising: Birth-Life-Death/Rebirth. This is the key to the evolution of the individual and of the ethnic unit.

3) Ancient Armanic cultural features were not wiped out by the coming of Christianity—but found refuge in the symbolism used by the church itself and in folk customs. Today these await decoding that they may once again live in their rightful place.

These tenets are further explained in S. E. Flowers' introduction to Guido von List's *The Secret of the Runes*. Examples of all of them can be found in the pages of Kummer's *Rune-Magic*.

The idea of "Ariosophy" as such also involves the Theosophical notion of there being an evolutionary process at the leading edge of which the "Aryan" stands. Ariosophy also includes the specific idea that there was a time period in which "god-men" and "beast-men" existed as separate species, but that at a certain time in the distant past they began to interbreed—resulting in the present form of homo sapiens. Ariosophy preaches the necessity of "breeding out" the "beast-man" characteristics to return to the former divine state of the "god-man."

There are several statements made, or sentiments expressed, by S. A. Kummer in the text of *Rune-Magic* which might be found to be "offensive" by the politically correct, and some that are factually erroneous. Rather than censoring Kummer, or arbitrarily editing him, we have translated his work as it stood in 1933. This is in keeping with the general editorial philosophy of the publisher not to "sanitize" controversial works. It is felt that the documents will have more historical, as well as intellectual, value if they are allowed to speak for themselves. Notes have been added to the text where warranted.

When translating any of the Ariosophical literature there are always problems regarding word-plays the original writers use, which may be impossible to represent in English terms. Where possible cognate translations are used which preserve the sound correspondences or word-play. But sometimes other solutions' must be found. Words appearing in square brackets [ ] are information not belonging to the translation proper but which has been included by the editor. This is often an original German word, the form of which may be helpful to the understanding of

2

the magical or poetic logic of the text. Or bracketed words may be etymological translations of certain "magical words" or names in the original German text. These measures have been found to be necessary in the translation simply because so much of the linguistic magic of the *Armanen* is dependent on similar sounding words or folk-etymological word-plays.

Edred Thorsson
Austin, Texas
February 1, 1993ev

Author's Introduction

Rune-magic is the great knowledge of cosmic energies, the recognition of hidden energies of nature, of the subtle heavenly, as well as earthly streams, waves, entities, and powers. All forms of higher wisdom, all secret knowledge of the world, are but fragments, and through the course of time have been for the most part distorted and corrupted; but at one time it had its origin in the divine, Aryan magic of the Runes. All languages of the world are derived from the Aryo- Germanic mother-tongue, which is both magical and alive. The Germanic Runic script is the script of all scripts. Runes are not just letters or verbal symbols, but primal symbols of a living magical nature which whisper to us. These may be experienced physically through Runic postures and dances and are useful for your own well-being and even for the blessing of all mankind. Whoever physically forms and experiences the Runes in a pure and conscious manner, will have great secrets opened to him, if he practices, vibrates, and dances in the radio waves, subtle currents and flowing energies of the All. Accompanying ideal higher development, clairvoyance, astral perceptions, heightened psychic ability and prophetic vision will arise in the Runer, in the practitioner.

In the small manuscript before you I can give only a few gems from the great treasure trove of Aryan wisdom and Rune-magic, but these will be of great use to the reader and will lead him into the Way of the Grail. To anyone who has greater interest in Runic history, magic and mysteries I recommend my work, *Heilige Runenmacht*.[1]

The following exercises and instructions may be undertaken only with noble and pure thoughts—the blessings of the Runes will not fail.

Hail him who learns it!
Hail him who teaches it!
Therefore take advantage of
The blessing, ye who hear it![2]

Alaf sig runa![3]   The Author

The 18-Rune Row

Other than the oldest Runic Futhork (alphabet), which has 18 runes and corresponds to the "Rune Poem" of the "Hávamál,"[4] there are various other Rune-rows.

Primarily the oldest, the 18-Rune, Futhork comes into consideration, for penetrating into higher Rune-wisdom, into the Runic mysteries, with the initiations they provide. The cosmic and magical legitimacy of this Futhork cannot be supplanted by any other Rune-row.

The 18-Rune Futhork-Alphabet

The f-Rune, *Fa*, Fa-tor = Father; generation in Spirit and in Matter, kindling a fire, fire- engendered magical force which shapes everything; the eternal return[5] of the Fa-tor—pure Love which constantly works in a creative manner. Numerical value 1.

The u-Rune, the *Ur* [primal, original], Rune of primal fire, original creation, primal birth, primal Spirit, original knowledge, primal light, original position, primal cause, original eternity, primal time, origin, original writing, judgment [or-deal], primal basis, original mother, the Norn *Urda*, Uranus, primal arising, primal being, primal passing-away.[6] The origin of all manifestations is the *Ur*- the *Ur* of the All, the *Ur* of the Earth. Urn. Numerical value 2.

The th-Rune, Thor; thurs, thorn. Thorn is Will and Deed. Donar = Don-Aar, the singing sun, the thunder, Thor's hammer. The Thorn of Fate, the Thorn of Life, but also the Thorn of Death which leads to rebirth; no Life without Death, no Death without Life. Sleeping Beauty, who is awakened by the Thorn of Life. The Gate (The Golden Gate and the Gate of Misfortune in folk tales.)[7] Numerical value 3.

The o-Rune, *Os*; East, Easter, Ostara, the goddess of Spring. *Os* is the rune of spiritual speech, of power, of language; through spiritual regeneration, every negative force can be overcome. *Os* = womb, *Osrun* which conceives—that which is conceived by Spirit and Love becomes a reality. Numerical value 4.

The r-Rune, *Rit*; counsel [rede], wheel [*Rad*], red, rita, rota— holy, invulnerable, innate Righteousness. Cosmic rhythm, whispering, raging, rolling, rubbing, rustling, etc. The Savior [*Retter*], the Righteous, the Rider [Knight], the Hero [*Recke*], Ararita, the Law, the symbol of the All-Rite. The Rune of Righteousness and Integrity. Numerical value 5.

The *k*-Rune, *Ka*, is the Rune of Cause and Effect, of poetic justice. Its sound, *k*, indicates to spiritual and physical ability, to cures, art [*Kunst*], those who can, king, queen, *Kun*, *Kano*, the canoe as a feminine symbol; Arkona, the Knowing One, the Norn. Kala,[8] the secret of traditional Knowledge. *Ka*, the Rune of pure, conscious, racial generation and multiplication. Numerical value 6.

The *h*-Rune, *Hagal*, Hag-All. All-Hag, God-All, Walhalla, World-All, Man-All; hedge, enclose, hem in, to hide within one's self, to include everything, the key to all rowning-Runes, to the great and holy All. The *Hagal*-Rune is the World Rune, the World-Tree, around the midpoint of which the whole spiritual and physical world revolves. The Rune of the holy seven, of sense, of sounds, of colors, of harmony, of the eternal wisdom in the divine, all- encompassing Self. Numerical value 7.

The *n*-Rune, *Not* [Need], *naut*, *nit*, is the Rune of Need and Death, necessity, the necessity of Fate; the Rune of the Norns who spin the threads of Fate. The compulsion of Fate, a necessity which a self-imposed trial by Need helps to unburden. Necessity guides the transformation to higher spiritual and astral levels, as well as to rebirth. Become a true helper and healer and thou wilt outgrow Need and Death. Numerical value 8.

The *i*-Rune, *Is*, I [Self],[9] is the Rune of the conscious Self, of self-mastery, of wise magic. It corresponds to the One, to Unity, to the great Union. The One is the most complete of all numbers; it also represents the divine, conscious human being.[10]

The *Is*-Rune is the ninth Rune in the Runic alphabet, and indicates the magical Nine of completion. It is the Rune of the upright, enterprising, conscious leader and magician. Its symbol is the World Axis, the Irmin-column = Irminsul. Numerical value 9.

The *a*-Rune, *Ar*, Aar [eagle], the Eagle of the Sun, nobleman, Aryan, Arman, the Son of the Sun. Aar- fire = primal fire, the Son of God. Harmony = Ar-mony. Ar = acre [field]. Ar- Arahari, the spiritual Sun; Arimann, the Sun-Man, the Aryan. The Ar-Rune is also the rune of the healer, the physician [*Arzt*]. Numerical value 10.

The *s*-Rune, Sig, Sal, Sol, the Rune of the Sun's power, of
victory [*Sieg*]; Sal and Sig = Well-being and victory; of the
Light, of the Hale, of the soul, of the kindling, lightning; *Sig* = the
sunlight; the Sieve, the Seventh (head of the ruling council), the
clan of blood-kin. The *Sig*-Rune is the rune of the fighter and the
victor; it provides victory and makes the enemy cowardly, weak
and powerless. Numerical value is 11.

The *t*-Rune, *Tyr*, is the Rune of good fortune, of spiritual
victory, of rebirth, of creation, but also of destruction and
eternal change; Thor, Tyr, Tiu, Zir, Teut. It is the Rune of the
Teut = Teut-ons = *Deut-sch* [Germans]. It indicates a concealment, disguise; also within it operate the Three: Arising-Being-
Passing away to new Arising– therefore turning, twisting, striving
ever upward. *Tyr*, the Third, the threefold power. The spiral current, the cosmic rhythm; the arrow- and lance-head in the shape
of the *Tyr*-Rune. Numerical value 12.

The *b*-Rune, *Bar*, bier, birth, bearing Life. *Bar* = song, Bard
= singer; revelation = birth of the Spirit. Bourn = spring,
spring of health; but also stretcher, bier, being imprisoned, leaking
away. *Bas*, the breast, the womb of the Mothers. The Rune of birth
and procreation, concealment, being hidden, burrowing. *Bar-bar-
baren*, that is, the thrice reborn. The *Bar*-Rune lays bare to us the
idea of Birth originating in primal Birth. Numerical value 13.

The *l*-Rune, *Laf*, lagu, laug, means Life, law of Life, liver,
restoration, lye, leaves, Lagu = sea, laughter, lake. Also,
love, loftiness, light, ardor [*Lohe*], light of Life, insight into Life, the
lantern, enlightenment, refreshment, loudness, spring-time [*Lenz*],
linden-tree, sorrow [*Leid*], lore; lead = learning. *Laf*, the Rune of
initiation, but also the Rune of experiences and examinations.

The *Luev*, *Leb*, *Lew*, lion. The heraldic beast of all Life is the
kalafied* *Laf*-Rune. Numerical value 14.

The *m*-Rune, *Man*, exhorts us and whispers to us that we
should become conscious of our inner God-spark, our higher
Selves. *Man*, the German leader who stems from Manus, from the
Spirit of God Himself (Dio = Teut = *Deutsch* = German), Son
of God. *Man*, the Rune of the breath, of truth, of power and the
positive force of mankind. The Rune of the Spirit and the Soul,
of the Body—of awakening, working, governing, passing away, of
arising anew spiritually—which the three limbs striving upward

---

* kala = Secret, concealment, [*Verdrehung*].[11]

also indicate. Manus is the mystical tribal father of the *Germanen* [the Germanic folk]. The mysterious Amen, Omen, Om are derived from the old Nordic, Germanic root *Man*, which means the God-man, the Spirit-Man. Numerical value 15.

The *y*-Rune, *Yr*, wrong, error, iris, yew tree. This Rune means misunderstanding, confusion, insanity, reversal, denial, destruction, overthrow, temptation, erroneous lust in love. The erring human, standing on his head. The Rune of erring love, of sorrow and of lust; joy and pain, laughing and weeping. Numerical value 16.

The *e*-Rune, *Eh, Ehe* [marriage] = eternal, the true, procreation, the Law of Nature, which is fulfilled between man and wife. The two Selves, two lives which by pure Love bind together themselves in marriage, merge, and through mutual spiritual and physical re-polarization attain a higher life. The *Ehe*-Rune is the great Rune of Love, which will in future times bring us to the zenith of our Germanic race.[12] Numerical value 17.

The *g*-Rune, *Gibor*, Ge, Gea, Geo = Earth, God, gift, giver, *Gibor*—the Rune representing the Fyrfos, the swastika, the fire of Love, constant re-creation and eternal rebirth. *Giboraltar*,[13] the altar of the All-Father, the Giver; the Giver-Rune, in which is contained the Mal- cross [the "times-sign"], the crossing, the marriage of two Selves, of two powers. *Gibor* is the Eternal in human hearts. *Gibur Arahari!* = Man, be one with God!—or—Give us primal power, Soul of the Sun, Arahari! Numerical value 18.

The Magical Rune-Circle

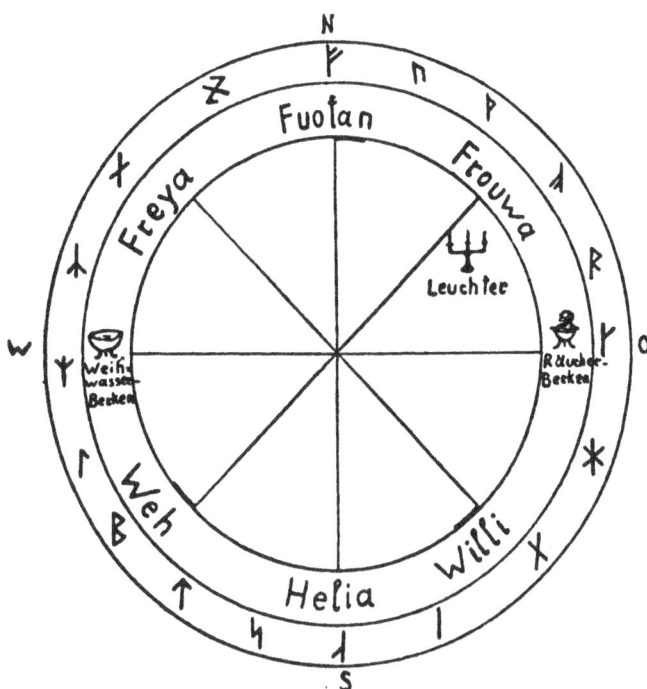

Magic circles should be drawn on the ground with green chalk, names and Runes with red chalk. The Runer should always begin in the North (Fa-Rune). The candlestick, holy water and censer are to be used only at night for magical consecrations. While drawing the magical Rune-circle, the Runer should meditate spiritually, recite a prayer or the Rune banishing.[14] When the drawing is completed the Runer should stand in the center of the circle, in which he can now move freely to devote himself to the Rune-postures, meditations, or Rune-signs, protected against bad influences, thoughts and currents. The Rune-circle is one of the most effective means of protection and defence for magical operations, as well as for Rune-postures and sensing the Runes. Upon completion of the exercise or magical operation, the Runer should thoroughly wipe away the circle from the inside outward, during which time he should again recite a prayer or the Rune banishing.

11

**Man-
Rune**

Form the M– grasp the Aethers,
As did thine Aryo-Germanic fathers,
Thou sensest in thee a whispering and singing,
Which to thee a holy message is bringing.

The Runer should take up the well-known basic military position (at attention)—the *Is*-Rune—facing North or East. The posture is erect, the chin is slightly drawn in, the back arched. The hands are held at the sides, the heels close together, toes pointed outward. Any rigid exaggeration of the posture must be avoided. The Runer should inhale and exhale deeply three times. With this exercise the Runer has to purify himself and ready himself for the reception of divine Rune-currents. He should raise both arms diagonally upward, so that he forms the human M-Rune, as shown in the drawing above. The palms are turned upward and slightly cupped.

The Runer should now begin to hum: *m-m-m*, to slow, deep breathing. You should begin soft and deep, let the tone swell and rise to the highest pitch, then sink slowly again to a deep tone. The *m* is to be hummed at all tone levels and in different volumes; it can also be sung in a siren-like fashion. You should imitate the humming of bees.

The whole formula is to be repeated for half an hour, with good, deep breathing. If your arms become tired, they can be held for short pauses in the *Is*-Rune position, during which time, however, you should continue to meditate spiritually on the reception of subtle cosmic energies.

The subtle currents of the All-power, like radio waves, flood into the back of the Runer's head, flow through the back and sympathetic nerves and gather in the solar plexus and around the navel. At the same time subtle waves of power flow into the palms of the hands (hand centers), flood through your arms, stimulate the thymus gland (in the center of the chest), join with the streams of the All-power in the sympathetic nerves, activate the spleen, and strengthen the gathered currents of power in the solar plexus, from where they fade away through the navel into the aura. To some extent, they also flow through the legs and then through the foot centers (in the middle of the feet) into the earth, into the place you are standing. This process is repeated throughout the entire practice session and brings about a strange, blissful, beautiful feeling—a fine ringing and vibration in the practitioner. The glands and higher centers of the body begin to sparkle; the inner Self is freed from the constricting bonds of the body; flashes of thought, ancestral memories and astral perception dawn from within the Runer.

You can feel and sense the cosmos, the world, in yourself whenever you hum the tones of the *Man*-Rune. Every Rune has a different type of current, a different strength, vibration, and rhythm. Those who understand it and learn to connect themselves consciously to the All-current of the *Man*-Rune become conscious magicians and masters of their Fates.

The *Man*-Rune may be felt in other related types of current by means of the following sound-formulas:

ma-me-mi-mo-mu
am-em-im-om um

After ending the exercise the Runer should drain off any energies which have been too strongly accumulated, or unfavorable waves accumulated through false thoughts, in the following manner:

In the *Man*-Rune posture, hum the *m* in a high tone, then sink to the lowest tone, while thinking, consciously willing, that all waves harmful to the Spirit, Soul and Body are bound to the tone vibrating in the body, and flow through the body and fade away under the soles of his feet into the earth with the deepest tone.

The Formation of the Grail-Chalice

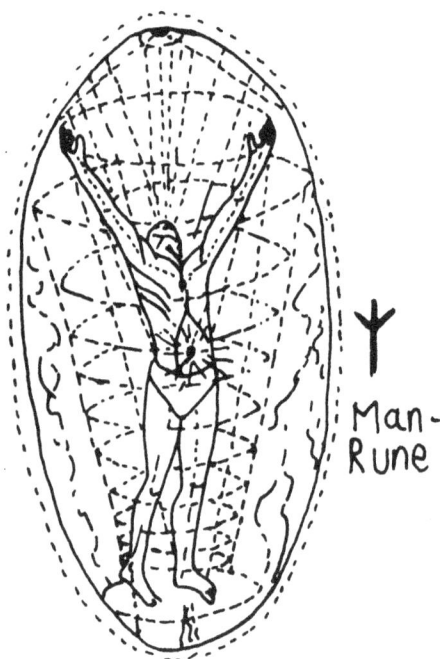

Man-Rune

The formation of the Grail-Chalice should only be attempted after the *Man*-Rune has been practiced for at least 20 minutes beforehand; otherwise the aura of the Runer will not be sufficiently charged with subtle energies, and the Runic antenna-net will not have been developed. This is absolutely essential for the formation of the Grail-Chalice.

The Runer should again strike the *Man*-Rune posture. The hands are stretched upward in the form of a chalice. The head is raised; the eyes directed serenely into the All. Your weight should be placed on the left foot, while the right foot rests lightly to the side. In this way the astral power centers of the body are most strongly activated. Due to this position, the Rune-stream, the subtle current of energy, is unable to dissipate sufficiently through just the one foot into the earth and seeks an escape through the navel into the aura, where it then, in conjunction with the fading energies from the mouth, forms the Grail-Chalice. Standing in this position the Runer will feel a rather strong prickling sensation in and around the navel.

Now the Runer should sing the formula: *O-o-m-m* rhythmically, like, for example, the chiming of church bells, while he imagines that from his mouth emanate rings of subtle energy which vibrate around his whole body and increasingly complete the Grail-Chalice, which finally results in a strong, magnetic center of Light which attracts higher, spiritual, cosmic influences. It is important for this mysterious exercise that a pure, noble state of mind be in control of desires and efforts toward Universal Love and higher development. During the singing you should think as follows:

> Fa-tor, I call to Thee,
> With All-power stream through me,
> The Grail in me awake,
> Threefold in Love a Tyr's oath I take.

Those well connected within the Cosmos are able to build around themselves a very strong Odic mist– the so- called "cape of invisibility" [*Tarnkappe*].[15]

In order to materialize the vibrating Grail-Chalice even more, the Runer should turn counterclockwise in a circle on the left foot. As you rhythmically sing the formula in various pitches and volumes, breathing deeply. In this position Runers receive counsel, knowledge and astral perceptions—according to their levels of development.

After ending the exercise, a good discharge of power is to be undertaken, as explained in the *Man*-Rune exercise. Finally, there follows a 10-minute pause of listening and waiting in inner peace and silence.

In the short text before you, I am unable to go into the further secrets concerning the formation of the Grail-Chalice—to seekers the foregoing will suffice for them to be able to penetrate further into this mystery of the Runes. Hail and Victory[16] to them on the Way of the Grail! The Grail is in its highest meaning nothing other than the holy vessel of the All, the self-contained All which pure Runers build around themselves.

> as thou art,
> so is thy Grail!

Runes—Yodels—Cheers

In old yodels and cheers we recognize the ancient Aryan name of god: Ja-Je-Jo-Ju.[17] This is the god of jubilation, of joy and yea-saying—but also the name for the Ju-Gu, Goths, or Nation of God. In yodels we recognize the Germanic Rune-cult, the sacred songs and battle yells of our forefathers, which have survived in our mountain regions to the present day. Yodels are linked to song-like melodies and are sung in specific arrangements of tone and word. There are no arbitrary aspects to these ancient traditional yodels, for they are connected to quite precise formulas— magical powers of the Runes and of words.

In olden times yodels were sung only together with specified bodily exercises—Rune postures and dances–which notably increased their magical effects. Yodels are a form of worship—Nature-bound prayer to the All-father—the one great God of the Worlds. Thus, our ancestors, in the highest affirmation of life, celebrated the *Yod-ler*, the *God-ler*, and the *Yell-er*, as a song of thanks and a prayer of joy to their God of Jubilation, the god Baal (Bal, Dur). Now, as millennia ago, yodels are sung by our Alpine dwellers and mountain-folk. Even if the deeper sense is lost to them, the powers of the Runes still work and produce in the yodler a great joy of life and an extremely close bond with nature, which helps our mountain folk through every hardship in life.

R. J. Gorsleben calls the *Ju-ra* Mountains, which extend throughout southern Germany, the center of the former cultic prominence of the god Ju. A very large number of old Ju-cult centers are still preserved.

I am convinced that in olden times yodels were practiced in the far north and in northern and central Germany. The yodels which have survived can only be regarded as remnants of old Germanic songs of sanctification, battle yells and songs of healing from a time long before the coming of Christianity. As a battle song they must have produced a colossal magical effect upon the enemy. In the magazine *Der Germane* (vol. 3), J. Nase writes the following:

" To support the view of the great age and the holy meaning of the yodel, I should like to refer here to the oldest historical evidence (next to the Tacitus passage)[18] available to me for their appearance; which to be sure, apparently speaks of yodels with word texts. It is to be found in the appendix of the work *Misopogon* by the later Roman Emperor Julian the Apostate, and reads in translation:

'So I saw the barbarians (in Germania) on the other side of the Rhine singing passionate tunes with words which resembled the cry of cackling hens, and (I saw) their joy in these songs.' Forgive me, if this translation is incorrect! On the basis of this passage, stories have always been told about how the singing of Germanic folk resembled the croaking of birds of prey."

Julian, who himself fought against the Germanic peoples, probably does not have in mind here the battle song of the Germanic tribes. In this case he would probably have said: "So I heard," instead of "So I saw." Because of this latter expression, as well as the emphasis on the joy of the Germanic people in these melodies described as being passionate, one begins to suspect that the passage deals with the observation of a legislative *Thing*-assembly of a Germanic tribe supporting the field commander, then allied with the Romans. His comparison of the reported manner of song with the cackling of hens, in spite of the apparently disparaging manner of expression of a foreign observer, is nonetheless quite vivid, and one can recognize in this an authentic description of yodeling, when one thinks about the first part of the stanza, arranged for several voices, with the long drawn out ending.

Since Julian's Germanic campaign obviously did not concern mountain people whose customs he was observing, his testimony may therefore further serve to establish the fact that yodeling as Runic and sacralized song was the expression of a widespread, common Germanic custom. Its present occurrence only among the residents of the Alps demonstrates to us the tenacity of the life-span of ancient Germanic ethnic treasures, which must be described as spiritual treasures. So, again, it is not difficult to recognize the manner of the *barditus*, or battle song, described by Tacitus in his *Germania* in part as yodeling. He writes:

"Further, they know such songs called *barditus*; through their utterance they quicken the spirit of battle, and from the song itself they prophesy the outcome of the coming engagement. As the song rises out of the ranks, they arouse fear or foster fear, and the song expresses, as it were, almost the beat of brave hearts as the joined sound of single voices. Primarily, it is in a raw tone and almost a muffled din. While singing, they hold their shields in front of their mouths to allow the sound to swell fuller and stronger through the echo." [19]

Through the previous exercises, new light falls on this famous passage.

Guido von List gives an enlightening explanation in his *Ursprache für die Jodlerart der Selbstlaute* [Primeval- Language for Yodeling the Vowels], as to how yodeling is involved with ancient Germanic customs. He directs our attention to the threefold mystical sense added in ancient times to the vowels A, E, I, O, U.[20] This idea still has echoes in the fact that a! is the outburst of amazement, of wonderment, but also of contempt. Likewise, e! is the cry of a sense of justice, of regret and of inhibition; i! is the cry of inwardness, of stress of the ego or of the individual personality, as well as of fear; while o! serves as the expression of pain, of aversion and of fear of death; as u! serves as a shout of joy and surprise, of spurring on to energetic endeavor, and as a cry of terror. The Germanic people were thoroughly shaped by mystical values.

This ancient sense of the vowels is again related to their mystical primal meaning as symbolic sounds, namely, *a* as the fundamental sound of the meaning of shaping [*Schaffen*] and mastering [*Walten*]; *e* as the fundamental sound of decreeing [*Gesetz*], ethics [*Recht*] and being [*Leben*]; *i* is the fundamental sound of inwardness, of spiritual light; *o* is the fundamental sound for the corporeal, for order; *u* is the fundamental sound for that which was perfected in the pre-temporal All-Perfected—the *Ur*- the Height, ruling from the Beyond.

These developments in the study of language strengthen the view that the age of yodeling reaches back deep into the earliest times of the Aryo-Germanic tribes.

Yodeling is also related to the time of the solstices, hence *hulen and julen*, Hail and Yule, as opposites, like struggle and victory. R. J. Gorsleben writes in his work *Die Hoch-Zeit der Menschheit* [Zenith of Mankind]:

"Hu is a high celestial god of the Aryo-Atlanteans, whom we find widespread in the divine syllables Ju, Jo, Ja, Je; who also is hidden in the names *Ju-ra* (the Ural mountains), *Ju-ropa* = Europa; also in the *Ju-hymns* to the *Ju-baal* = the Jubilee-God of the Alpine folk, in the cheers and yodels (Godly songs), in the *Hul* and *Jul* [Yule], the two solstices, with their annual feasts. In the old village of Freesen in Thuringia, at the time of the Summer Solstice, the young girls call to the young men: 'Hihu!' and the latter reply in a deep voice: 'Hexe!' [witch!] In other places they call: 'Yuhu!'"

18

In the word *yodel* the name of God—Yott is present, still unadulterated. Our German word *Ja* [yea], the affirmation, the affirmative movement, went out with the waves of Aryan conquerors and became the divine name Ya-weh, Yeho-va, Yo, Ya, Ye, Yuh. The word "Yu-hu," in which both divine names are connected, contains the expression of the absolute highest affirmation of Life which is in the Divine. The syllables Yo-Go also express Life and Movement and became the priestly name of Jona, "going," English "to go"; those traveling the Sun's path in the holy circles of stone of the island of Jo-na, an Atlantean nucleus in Scotland. In the Celtic regions of Ireland and Scotland, Hu-man was principally honored.

Man = God, therefore Hu-Man is the Hu-God, and his servants are the hu-mans. The German clan names of *Huch* and the English "Hugh," "Hughes," etc., refer to the "Hug-est," the Highest.[21]

Jugend [youth] is easily explained from a combination of *Ju* and *gend, kent*, from the *Kun*-Rune—therefore that which "kunnt" = comes directly from God.

This is closely related to Ith—Jud—Juda, which also means "stemming from God," Ju-da; likewise, the Goda, the Goth, who is "godly." The Jews stole this Germanic name, to which they have no right, for it is purely a German word, the *Jude*, the Good, the Goth.[22]

"Ach, Herr Je!" is part of the invocation to Ja, not a suppressed outburst, "Ach, Herr Jesus!" [Oh, Lord Jesus!].

In the "Holdrio" of the yodel is still contained the invocation of the *Hol-trio*, the Holy Three, to whom was also consecrated the *Hol-under*, the elder-tree, the holy tree.

Some old yodels which have been handed down are given below. To anyone who might be interested in further examples I recommend the worthwhile collection by Prof. Dr. J. Pommer: *Jodler und Juchzer mit Notendruck* [Yodels and Cheers with Musical Notation].

The circle above the *a* in the following yodels indicates a deep a-sound, which stands in the middle between the High German *a* and *o*.[23] By *Juchzer, Jauchzer* and *Juchzer* [cheers], we mean calls which come very close to being musical, but which stand somewhere between yodels and inarticulate cries. When one shouts a yodel or cheer into the mountains and cliff walls, the short passage of notes rings out, and like the distant sound of an organ, the threefold tone—repeated many times in its component parts—echoes back in alternating play from near and far. For you, dear readers, I hope that at least one of the following yodels may become a faithful companion to you in life. It will ever call forth in you a feeling of contentment and joy and will help you easily overcome anything which is difficult in life, and will generate in you a constant bond with the All and a strong feeling of hope. It will maintain your youthfulness and health well into the most advanced age. By means of yodling you drink from a divine, cosmic goblet magical Rune-powers, rich in blessings, so that your soul celebrates and cheers for happiness.

While singing the yodel I recommend to anyone who is to some extent familiar with the Runes—as it may suit the individual—to take up the appropriate Runic posture. Also it is good, while singing, to stretch your arms out to your sides and to dance slowly in waltz-step in a circle. In any event the effect will not be lost if you merely sing the yodel.

1. From St. Radegrund am Schöckl near Graz; Stiermark.

Ri - de - ra ridl idl a di - ri - di

ridl a di - ri - di ridl a da ri - da - ra idl idl

a di - ri - di ridl adl idl a

2. From Alt-Aussee, Stiermark. Received from the Forester Gruber on the Mondsee.

Hål ja hål djä i i a i i jä i idi

hål ja hål djä i i a i i i å

3. From Fuchsl, Salzburg (1888).

Jä di ri di jä i ti ri di ri ti ri ti ti

jä di ri di jä i ti ri di ri ti ti

4. Yells. Calls from the Offensee collected 1886.

1. I ⌣ juch!

2. Ju ju ju ju ju!

3. I ⌣ jä de rä!

4. Ju hu hu!

5. Ju hu hu hu hu!

6. I ⌣ u hu!

7. I ⌣ ju hu hu hu hu!

Runic Hand-Signs

Here I present for the first time the sensing of Runes and the activating of certain magical Runic power through hand positions and signs. These powers can not be misused, since they only become manifest to the Runer who strives toward higher development. The procedure is similar to the Rune postures, except that here a strong collection of subtle energies in the hand centers is reached. The person fully familiar with the experience of the Runes* will, as his body is already well saturated with the energies of the Runes, reach further understanding and perception in a short time. In the same way, the beginner is led by consciously directed will, patience and persistence toward the goal.

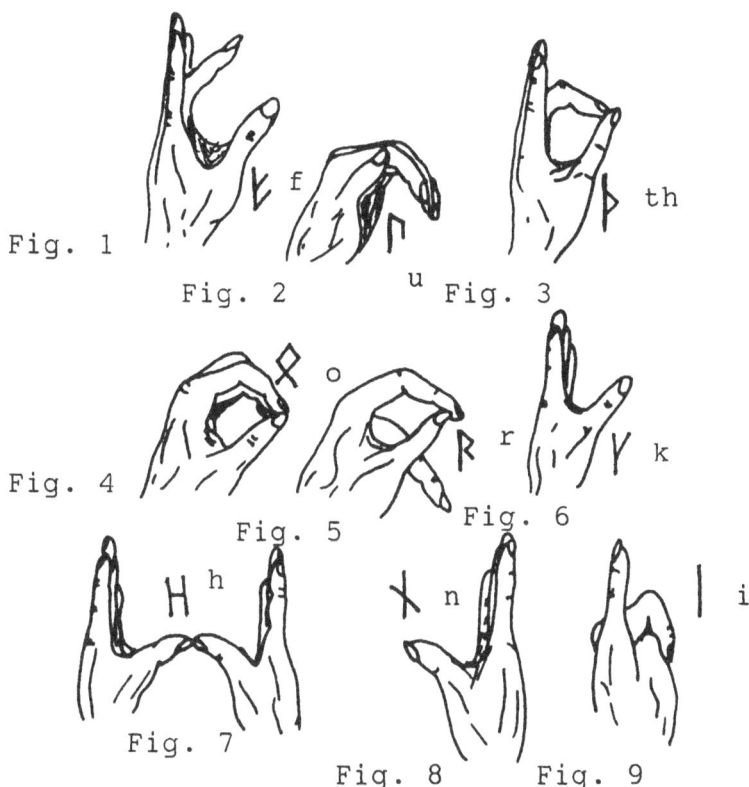

Fig. 1

Fig. 2   f

u   Fig. 3   th

Fig. 4

o

Fig. 5   r   R

k   Fig. 6

h   H

n   i

Fig. 7

Fig. 8   Fig. 9

---

* See my work *Heilige Runenmacht*. Hamburg: Uranus, 1932.

Fig. 10 a

Fig. 11 s

Fig. 12 t

Fig. 13 b

Fig. 14 l

Fig. 15 m

Fig. 16 e

Fig. 17 g

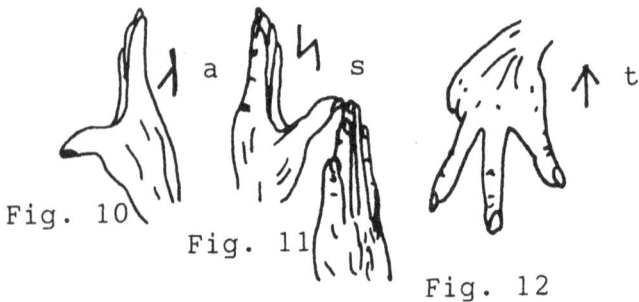

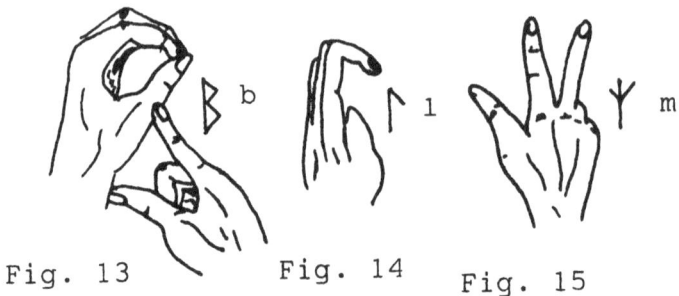

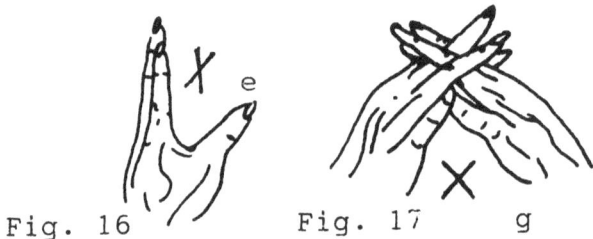

The *f*, *Fa*-Rune. The Runer should take up the *Is*-Rune position (military attention); then follow this with three cycles of deep breathing exercise, during which your thoughts are directed toward physical and spiritual cleansing. This practice should also be observed before performing all the other Rune signs. Now raise your left arm straight up, and put your left hand in the position shown in Fig. 1 in the sketches given in the tables above—forming the *Fa*-Rune. With good deep breathing, sing *f-f-a-a*, rising from the deepest to the highest tone, lets the voice sink to the middle tone and rise again to the highest; and repeat the singing in this position for three minutes. Immediately following take a short pause in the *Is*-posture, then the whole exercise is repeated twice more. Meanwhile your thoughts should be focused upon the unfolding primal fire, on the generation of fire, on fire-generated magical power, on pure Love for the Fa-tor of all Worlds. By the third repetition the Runer will detect a strong prickling sensation in the middle of the left hand—this is the emerging primal fire. With daily repetition the entire glandular system and bodily centers are stimulated to such an extent that the collection of energies continuously increases in the left hand and produces a real burning sensation. Your hand will begin to appear to turn red, and often it will vibrate with glowing red rays, during which time it may happen that astral perceptions will appear, images will be seen, and voices will be heard, etc. These appearances will be different for individual Runers depending entirely upon the composition of their blood[24] and their spiritual development.

By a conscious act of will the Runer should now, while singing from the highest to the deepest tones, circulate those energies gathered in his hand throughout his entire body. I shall give no instructions concerning the magical employment of this sign against other persons, but advise every Runer to use these signs only for his own development.

For this Rune hand-sign I give the following sound formulas: fa-fe-fi-fo-fu.

Fig. 2 shows the *Ur*-Rune hand-sign. Your left arm is bent below the shoulder height, so that the hand position, Fig. 2, comes to rest about 8 inches in front of your eyes. The Runer sings *u-u-u* in different pitches and volumes for three minutes, following which you take a short pause. Each Rune sign must be repeated three times for three minutes each, since otherwise no satisfactory collection of energies can be reached in the hand centers.

Inner meditation is focused on the intake of primal power, primal knowledge, increasing magical, magnetic powers.

Here the Runer will detect, above all in the finger-tips and the center of the hand, a certain cool, lukewarm, or even warm feeling. The perception is different for every Runer; as in every case of magnetism, one feels a coolness, another warmth, because every human being is polarized differently. The one is more electric, the other more magnetic, and as a result the perception varies as well.* At the end of the exercise, the Runer should circulate the collected energies by a conscious act of will throughout the entire

---

* Here I should like to mention the worthwhile investigations of

body, during which time advanced students can observe a pale gold-orange or gold-green oscillation of their auras. A strong charge of electro-magnetic powers can be achieved through this Rune hand-sign especially.

I recommend the following sound formula:

U-u-r-r.

Fig. 3. The Runer proceeds as with the *Fa*-Rune, stretches the left arm upward and takes the hand position of Fig. 3. Sing *d-a-a* three times, for three minutes each, during which higher tones are to be held longer. Here, too, cosmic energies begin to collect in the hand, which is experienced as prickling in the extended finger-tips, as well as in the ring finger and the tip of the thumb. Thoughts are focused on the reception of Solar powers. After ending the exercise the collected energies are to be circulated throughout the entire body by an act of conscious will. At the deepest tone they are focused in the feet. The astral color vibration is bright yellow. Also higher astral laws can be evoked by means of this hand-sign. This depends entirely on how much cosmic energy the Runer is able to absorb and take into the body. The deeper the inner concentration is, the stronger the collection of powers will be. Due to a lack of space I cannot do into further details here.

This Rune-sign also has the following sound formulas:

de-di-do-du.

Fig. 4. Here, too, the Runer proceeds as with the previous exercises—bend the thumb and forefinger of the extended hand so that the fingertips touch, as Fig. 4 shows. Sing the *o-o-o*-formula in the manner already explained. Soon you will feel a circulating vibration of energies in your hand. Then proceed as already explained for the previous signs. This is the sign of Odem, Ode and breath. This has an effect especially rich and in spiritual blessings for the conscientious Runer. Often after this exercise the smell of ozone can be detected from the hand. The astral color vibration is bright violet.

Fig. 5 shows the *Rit*-Rune hand-sign. The Runer should observe the previously stated methods by raising the left arm, assuming the hand position of Fig. 5, and purring *r-r-r* in siren fashion (i.e. with rising and falling tone and volume, as in the previous exercises). Inner thoughts are focused on higher counsel, on in-born right and cosmic rhythm. This Rune hand-sign produces a

---

J. P. Reimann Mar-Galittu on polarity and emanation research.

26

rhythmic warming of the hand and makes possible the engagement in the cosmic World-rhythm through which the higher centers are strongly stimulated and magical abilities unfold in the Runer. Also, a conscious, willed circulation of the power through the entire body should not to be neglected here. As astral vibrational colors I was able to detect various colors, e.g. whitish-yellow, pink, fire red, orange.

Further sound formulas of the *Rit*-Rune are:

ra-re-ri-ro-ru.

Fig. 6 is the *Ka*-Rune hand-sign. The aforementioned techniques apply here as well. The Runer sings *k-a-a-a*—inner meditation is on spiritual and physical balance, on higher ability and spiritual creativity. This hand-sign earnestly practiced brings about a feeling of becoming physically freer and lighter. After ending the exercise I could often detect a sulfur-like smell on the fingertips of my left hand.[25]

The color vibration is white to ivory. Further sound formulas are:

ke-ki-ko-ku.

Fig. 7. Here both hands are employed, as the sketch in Fig. 7 shows. The arms are stretched well upward. While the *h-a-a-a* sound is sung, special attention should be given to good, deep breathing—in other regards the previously stated instructions apply. This sign is a very strong conductor, so that one has the feeling as if an electric current were passing through the body. With deep concentration (deep-level consciousness), astral perceptions and higher inner experience enter the mind. This hand-sign is a strongly whispering Rune-sign. Thoughts are meanwhile focused on Universal Love, cosmic correspondences, animated by the desire for highest fulfillment.

After ending this exercise you will be able to detect a strong odor of ozone and sulfur on the index and middle fingers.

Color vibration is glowing indigo blue.

Further sound formulas:

he-hi-ho-hu.

Fig. 8. For this sign the Runer should use the right hand. Otherwise, the instructions already stated continue to apply. The Runer should hum the *n-n-n* sound siren-fashion. Thoughts are focused on higher development and attainment of perfection. The *Not*-Rune sign takes effect more spiritually and through the soul—

27

it allows your own need to be recognized, helps toward changing this need, and diminishes the ordeal involved. You will often perceive a cool, lukewarm or warm feeling in your hand, similar to that of the *u*-Rune. The astral color is dark red.

Further sound formulas:

na-ne-ni-no-nu.

Fig. 9 gives the *Is* or *I*-Rune hand-sign. The Runer should ball his left hand up, stretch the index finger out and sing from deep to high tone the *i-i-i* sound repeatedly. Thoughts are focused on Universal Love and the development of magical powers of the Self. In this sign you strongly feel the influx of cosmic energies into the tip of your index finger—the entire hand becomes warm. During the circulation through the body, you sense a warm stirring through the whole Self. After ending the exercise you can ascertain on the index finger a sulfuric smell (like burned gunpowder). I noticed that this smell is often different, but always sulfurous in nature. The astral color is blue to red-violet. This sign can also be formed with the right hand; it produces then a different body current which is to be recommended equally.

Fig. 10 shows the *Ar*-Rune hand-sign which is performed right-handed and with the thumb bent downward as far as possible. Here through singing the *a-a-a* sound particularly electric energies are accumulated in the hand, so that the Runer feels a fine tingling and a gentle prickling in the thumb, the base of the thumb, and the hand center; the outstretched fingers begin to vibrate lightly. Thoughts or inner meditations are focused on receiving *Ar*-Fire and Solar powers. This sign particularly affects the forces of life, in a rejuvenating and strengthening manner. Drawing the power into the body produces a strong effect on the solar plexus. The astral color is silver-grey to bright grey-green.

Fig. 11 portrays the *Sig*-Rune hand-sign, which is performed with the left arm extended (like the *Ka*-Rune sign, Fig. 6) and the right arm slightly bent, with the fingers closed and extended. The left thumb touches the tip of the index finger of the right hand.

Its sound formulas are:

S-s-i-g

sa-se-si-so-su.

Inner thoughts are focused on victory over one's own mistakes and weaknesses, on receiving sunny, victorious healing powers and the inherited memory[26] of magical might and power. By this hand-sign, too, a great accumulation of cosmic energies is acquired in the hands. The left hand becomes warm, and the Runer will feel how the current also passes into the right hand. During the discharge process, the current can be observed throughout the entire body. Here, too, one may detect an ozone odor coming from the hands. This sign produces a strong awareness of power and victory in the practitioner. With sufficient development of the Runer, higher magical laws will come into force.

The astral color is golden yellow by day, silver grey by night.

Fig. 12. The *Tyr*-Rune hand-sign is performed right-handed about 8 inches in front of the body, with a bent arm, so that the tip of the index finger is located at the height of the navel. The sound formulas are:

T-y-r

ta-te-ti-to-tu.

Spiritual meditation: "From rebirth to rebirth I have gone; I strive to Thee, All-Father; over Life and Death, through Sorrow, Stress and Need, Joy and Contentment I strive in longing back to Thee."

After several repetitions of this sign, the Runer will be able to perceive a pleasant turning or boring feeling in the right hand. A subtle bond develops with the navel, though which the energies affect the solar plexus, in such a way that a whispering begins in the Inner Self of the Runer, inherited memories and often astral perceptions appear.

The astral color is reddish grey by day, grey-blue by night.

Fig. 13. The *Bar*-Rune sign is produced with the arms raised above the head, as Fig. 13 shows. Its sound formulas are:

B-a-r

ba-be-bi-bo-bu.

Inner thoughts are focused on the birth of the Spirit and higher magical powers. Here the Runer, if inwardly well centered, will observe in the hands, as well as with the intake of power into the body, a light fluttering feeling, as if the higher Spirit and higher magical abilities were being born—engendered by the energies from this Rune-sign. Often, after weeks of daily practice, the feeling appears more strongly perceptible. Persistence leads to the goal.

The astral color is bright blue by day, bright violet by night.

Fig. 14 shows the *Laf*-Rune hand-sign. The Runer should raise the left arm upward and assume the hand position shown in

Fig. 14. Utilize the following sound formulas with this sign:

L-a-f

la-le-li-lo-lu.

Thoughts are focused on Love for the Fa-tor, on enlightenment of the Self. Here the Runer will observe a mild warming of the left hand. After ending this exercise I was able, on a number of occasions, to detect an odor similar to rubber. With this sign one is able to effect a strengthening of his aura. It is also the sign for initiation into higher Life.

The astral color is bright fire-red by day, ruby-red by night.

Fig. 15. The *Man*-Rune hand-sign is performed with the right arm stretched upward, with the hand position as shown in Fig. 15. Its sound formulas are:

m-m-m

M-m-a-n-n

ma-me-mi-mo-mu.

Thoughts are meanwhile focused on Universal Love, cosmic spiritual creativity and the awakening of divine magic. This sign is one of the most effective Rune-signs—the right hand begins to flame and glow. The Runer will have a sensation as if fine rays are emanating from three fingers, and the entire hand is strongly charged electrically. With this sign the Runer is prepared to banish every danger. It is the sign of the reborn, conscious magician and of the three-fingered Hand of Light of our exalted ancestors, which blesses and protects. This sign enables the Runer to penetrate into the highest secrets of Rune-magic. After performing this hand-sign, the aroma of burned electrical wires is often perceptible. Again it should be mentioned, as with all the hand-signs, the exercise should be concluded with the circulation of power through your entire body.

The astral color is purple-red by day, phosphorescent greenish-red by night.

Fig. 16 shows the *Eh*-Rune hand-sign[27] which is performed with the left hand, similar to the *Ka*-Rune sign, except that the thumb is spread somewhat further outward. Its sound formulas are:

e-e-e

E-h-e.

Inner thought is focused on pure Love, spiritual, psychic fusion, on freedom from low-minded drives and passions. This sign produces a pure and noble life in both thoughts and desires. With this sign a subtle wreath of light may be observed about the entire hand.

The astral color is yellow by day, yellow-green by night.

Fig. 17. In this sign the hands are folded above the head, except that the fingers remain stiff, straight and pointed. The sound formulas are:

ga-ge-gi-go-gu.

Thought is focused on the universal bond among all things, on the connection to the harmonious vibration throughout the All. This sign is also well suited to meditations and prayers. Spiritual clarity and a contented feeling of being safe and of inner peace is attained through this sign especially; inherited memories and high Aryan knowledge become apparent to the knowledgeable Runer.

The astral color is golden yellow by day, red-golden by night.

Gibur-Arahari!

To all practitioners Victory- and All-Rune Hail!

Important Glands and Higher Centers
of the Body

Explanation for the accompanying diagram

1 and 1a: Pineal gland (receiving centers)
2: Forehead centers (receiving-influence)
3 and 3a: Inner ear centers (clairaudience)
4 and 4a: Parotid glands
5 and 5a: Tear ducts
6 and 6a: Eyes, receiving and sending centers (clairvoyance)
7: Chin centers and lingual gland
8: Submaxillary gland
9: Thyroid gland
10 and 10a: Shoulder centers, sebaceous glands
11: Thymus gland
12 and 12a: Sweat glands
13: Cardiac sympathetic nerve
14: Sympathetic nervous system
15 and 15a: Elbow and inner arm centers (receiving)
16: Spleen
17: Pancreas
18 and 18a: Hip centers
19: Solar plexus
20: Navel (sending and receiving center)
21 and 21a: Hand centers
22: Sexual organs (polar centers, receiving, discharge)
23 and 23a: Knee and inner leg centers
24 and 24a: Foot centers (discharge)

On the outer right side the astrological signs are indicated. The arrows going out from these signs point to the part of the body ruled by each sign. The dotted oval around the drawing indicates the aura, the psychic cloak.

Additionally, I will mention that a great part of the development of higher powers and magical abilities depends on the heart and kidneys (adrenal glands). The well-known proverb: "To try someone by heart and kidneys" [*Jemand auf Herz und Nieren prüfen*], meaning "to test someone through and through" comes from this.

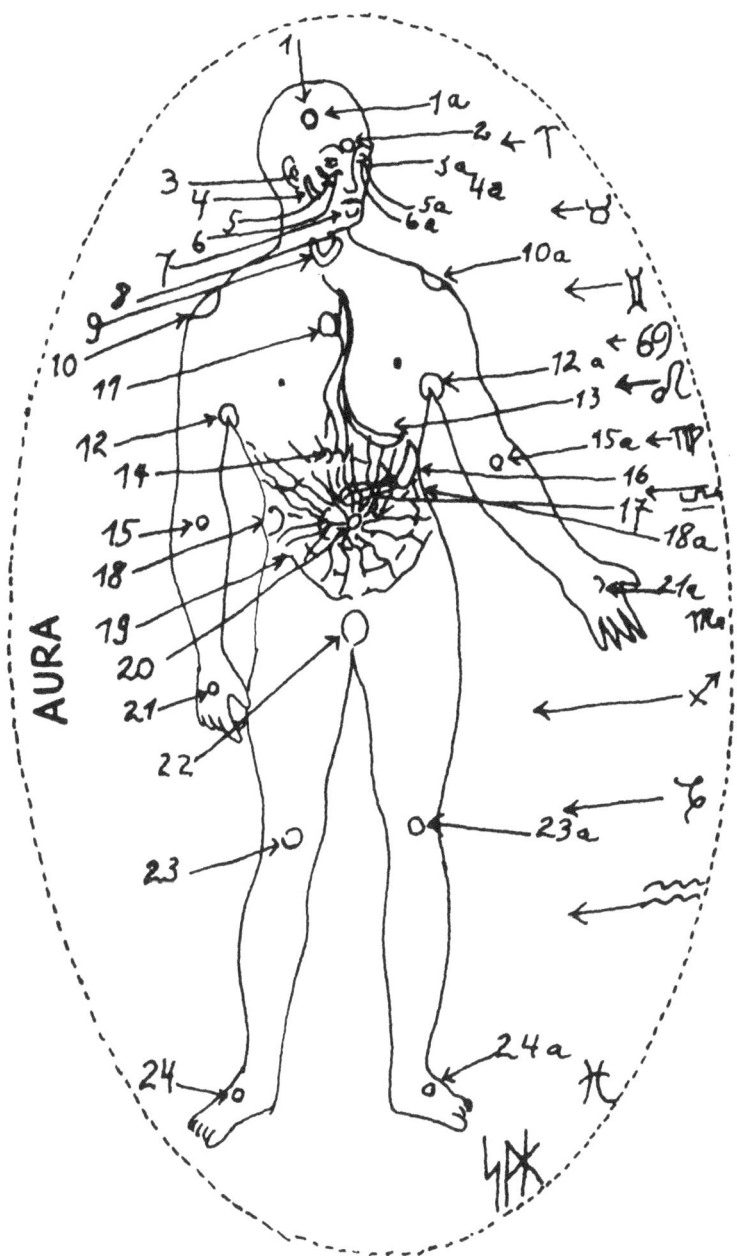

AURA

1
1a
2 ← ♈
3
4
5
6
7
8
9
10
11
12
14
15 → o
18
19
20
21
22
23
24

3a
4a
5a
6a
10a
12a ← ♋
13
15a ← ♍
16
17
18a
21a
♏
← ♐
← ♑
23a
← ♒
24a
♓

♉
♊

33

Magical Rune Formulas

Below I give several Rune-formulas passed down from ancient times, but I advise every Runer who may perhaps utilize them to approach such work most carefully; everyone is personally responsible for his own actions. The conscious and noble Runer will never reject laws or utilize powers whose effect he does not understand and has not sufficiently tested. Let no one misuse unknown magical formulas on his blood-brothers and sisters—he could not escape the avenging might of the Runes. Whosoever carves Runes, let him carve them in wood; whoever writes them, let him write them on paper, so they can be burned[28] at any time. Spiritual meditation is always important for the carving and writing of Runes.

Formula: *suf* or *fus* produces tiredness and sleep.

Formula: *sof* or *fos* produces forgetfulness and calming.

Formula: *Sig-Tyr* works positively, brings victory, happiness, strengthens the life force. This formula should always be used threefold.

Formula: *alu* or *ula* effects a defence, banning the enemy.

Formula: *Ara-hari* gives Solar force and effects protection against all dark powers.

Formula: *flu* or *ulf* produces cosmic Love.

Formula: *tuwatuwa* works as a ban and protection against black magical influence, against revenge, hate and envy.

Formula: *olu* or *ulo*—Spiritual power being proclaimed out of the *Ur* [origin].

Formula: *ul*—wisdom, primal life, primal Love.

Formula: *uste* produces a feeling of hope, the power of desire.

Formula: *ttt* brings understanding of Arising, Being, Passing away, Arising anew.

As a most powerful formula for banishing evil, one utilizes the entire Futhork, written once left to right and once underneath right to left.

The formula *ssgg* is the Divine Secret which holds the highest Jurisdiction. In ancient times this formula was called: "String, Stone, Grass, Groan" [*Strick, Stein, Gras, Grein*], and indicated "Jurisdiction, Secret, Accusation, and Judgment."[29]

These formulas may suffice as inspiration—further ones can be drawn easily from the Runic Futhork.

Sensitive Runers looking with astral vision by means of Rune-magic see with an abstract clarity, but they must primarily clarify that which they see for themselves. Whether they see in pictures or symbols, or sense or hear things of the past, present or future by astral means, correct interpretations will only be available to them once they have reached the higher stage of Rune-magic.

They should never forget that even the Runes have their demon; and one caught up in egoistic, lower thoughts and desires runs considerable danger of falling prey to this demon. Iron will, strict self-discipline, unshakeable faith in, and Love for, the All-Father, the Spirit of the World, make them true Seers—Sons of God.

The path upward to the Peak, to the Light, is difficult, so much purer and greater the magical might. Dear Blood Brother, guard yourself against the way into the depths; it is easier, more inviting, but also more devilish, because it brings you destruction.

Many a man went to Work some years ago with the best of intentions, but their animalistic, egoistic drives got the upper hand. Today they work as black magicians, and so they are ending up as destroyers through the might of the Runes.[30]

Bearing Womb of the highest Good
Continue to sustain us,
Eternal spring of racially pure Blood,
Strengthen us, we Aryan figures.[31]

卐　　　Arehisosur[32]　　卐

All-Fator's symbolic Counsel-Head, or Hari-Fuotan, within the Solar Circle. It is the head which again witnesses to us of majestic Fuotanism, Armanism—the faith of our fathers and forefathers.

Morning Consecration[33]

Most holy Fuotan, All-Father,
Thou, who art eternally threefold in, around, and above me,
I consecrate my Self, my Life, anew in true Love to Thee;
free me, cleanse me from everything base and impure,
let Divine Love, Wisdom and Will flow through my Self,
so that I may lessen my Garma;[34]
because my heart, my blood calls out to the Sun, Arahari,
to Thee!
Guard me against evil, dark powers and racial guilt,[35]
give me Love, joy in being, happiness and patience.
Through Thy Divine Triad my heart glows,
over Arising-Being-Passing away I stream sunward.
For Thy mercy eternal thanks;
I have reached understanding through whispering Runes.
I strive heroically nearer to Thee,
therefore forgive even me!
Sig-Tyr, Sig-Tyr, Sig-Tyr!

(S.A.K.)

Evening Consecration

Holy, great, almighty, triune Fuotan! I greet Thee and consecrate my Self to Thee anew. I thank Thee for Thy protection and Thy goodness; guard me against everything wicked, low and foreign. May Thy noble, merciful Father-Spirit forgive me my faults if I have erred; help me to overcome them and to make amends through noble deeds. Thy shelter and protection is my weapon against all enemies and dark forces, because Thou art my threefold Salvation, Sun and Light. I know no terror, no fear and trembling, because I am immune and invulnerable through Thee. Thou art the Love, the Truth, the Goodness, the Right. Thou art my longing and my sanctuary. Fuotan, almighty Father and World-Spirit, I call to Thee; I speak and fight for Thy Kingdom, so that darkness may vanish from the race and from the Fatherland.

Should the hour of my transformation be near, be Thou merciful, as to my forefathers, even to me.

Fuotan, Willi and Weh, I bless Thee, I greet Thee!

(S.A.K.)

Rune Banishing

All-Fator, Fuotan, I call to Thee!
With magic All-power flood me.
Awaken the Runes, the old lore, in me,
in holy Love I strive toward Thee.
With runic force I ban every wicked wight,
because I serve Thy godly might.
– alu – tuwatuwa – Arahari – Fuotan.

At the consecrated well of Urda the Norn
Silent I sat, I saw and mused.
Then heard I the speech of the High One.
Of the Runes he spoke, of counsel of the gods,
Of carving the Runes, of the whispering the Runes.[36]

Explanation of the Picture
on page 39

The high holy Grove of Light: Runa—the Divine Secret. Through the Gate which leads into this whispering grove, one sees the shadowless God-Man, Son of the Sun, highly developed through overcoming Self, vibrating in a cosmic sea of light and radiation. Before the Gate are two Germanic marking stones which open only to the Germanic adept who masters the higher mysteries, and who knows the secret of gravity. In the foreground stands the struggling Germanic man in the Not-Rune posture; he has recognized the High Way and is fighting through to the true Light by overcoming his own Need. He is, however, still a shadow-man; the most difficult test still lies before him.

Editor's Notes

(1) *Heilige Runenmacht* remains untranslated. Originally published by the Uranus Verlag in Hamburg, 1932.

(2) Based on the "Hávamál" stanza 165.

(3) This is a magical formula in the heraldic language of Guido von List. Its meaning is: "All victory for those conscious of the Divine Secret."

(4) See the "Hávamál" stanzas 138-165 in the *Poetic Edda*.

(5) Here the Nietzschean formula *ewige Wiederkehr* is used.

(6) The significance of the formula of Arising-Being-Passing away to new arising [*Entstehen-Sein-Vergehen-zum neuen Entstehen*] is an important one developed by G. v. List.

(7) From the tale of *Frau Holle* in the collection by the Brothers Grimm.

(8) *Kala* is a Sanskrit word borrowed by Guido von List to indicate the secret of the systematic permutations of esoteric meanings of words.

(9) Here the first person pronoun, *ich*, "I," is used as a noun—which is how Sigmund Freud referred to the Ego in German terminology: *das Ich*, "the 'I.'" The concept of the "ego" for the Armanen is a more comprehensive one involving the entire Self.

(10) Here and in the following section Kummer betrays the Neoplatonic basis for many of his underlying ideas.

(11) The practice of *kala* involves certain permutations of the meanings of words which conceal their meanings from the uninitiated. See note 8 above.

(12) This is an obvious reference to the quasi-mystical eugenic dreams common among contemporary Ariosophists.

(13) *Giboraltar* identified by Guido von List as the rock of Gibraltar.

(14) The texts of these prayers and Rune banishing are given on pages 34 and 35.

(15) The *Tarnkappe* plays a part in the German national epic, the *Nibelungenlied*, where it is part of the Nibelungen treasure won by the hero Siegfried by killing the serpent, Fafnir.

(16) *Heil und Sieg*—of course, these words were combined into the National Socialist chant, which they had borrowed from the

"mantra" of the *Germanen Orden.*

(17) Through this whole discussion of the consonant-vowel combinations with Ja-, etc., it should be remembered that the German /j/ is pronounced as the English /y/.

(18) Tacitus *Germania* chapter 10.

(19) Tacitus *Germania* chapter 3.

(20) These vowels have the sound values in English of *ah, eh, ee, oh, oo* respectively.

(21) This is folk-etymologically incorrect: Hugh is derived from the Germanic word **hug-:*'mind; shining'.

(22) Here Kummer expresses a kind of thinking common in Germany in 1932—in the time just before the assumption of power by the Nazis in that country.

(23) For English speakers this sound is best described as a deeper version of the /a/ in the word "call."

(24) Here we have another example of the particular occult ideology common among German rune magicians of the early 20th century. The *Blutsverfassung,* composition of the blood, is an obvious reference to the "purity of the blood" as measured by contemporary racial standards.

(25) See Sebottendorf's Sufi exercises in his book *Die geheimen Übungen der turkischen Freimauer* for reports of similar phenomena.

(26) This "inherited memory" [*Erberinnerung*] is something which one inherits from one's ancestors along meta-genetic lines.

(27) Notable for its absence is the *Yr*-Rune sign. Which apparently Kummer thought of as being too negative to be practiced.

(28) The runes are deactivated by burning them.

(29) See G. v. List's *The Secret of the Runes,* pp. 89–90.

(30) This seems to be a reference to the Nazi regime just coming to power as Kummer wrote this work.

(31) "Aryan figures" is used here as the translation of the original *Ariergestalten.* The word *Gestalt,* meaning basically "shape" or "form" was used at this time by Ariosophical ideologues to mean "an ideal type."

(32) *Arehisosur* is a formula made up of the Armanic names of the runic vowels: *Ar-eh-is-os-ur* = A-E-I-O-U.

(33) These "Consecrations" were written by Kummer to act

as morning and evening devotional prayers for his Runers to use in their daily meditational work.

(34) *Garma* is a special Ariosophical form of the Sanskrit word *karma*.

(35) Rassenschuld implies the concept of miscegenation.

(36) Based on the stanza 111 in the "Hávamál" found in the *Poetic Edda*.

Bibliography

Gorsleben, Rudolf John. *Die Hoch-Zeit der Menschheit.* Leipzig: Kohler & Amelang, 1930.

Hollander, Lee M., trans. *The Poetic Edda.* Austin: University of Texas Press, 1962, 2nd ed.

Kummer, Siegfried Adolf. *Heilige Runenmacht: Wiedergeburt des Armanentums durch Runenübungen und Tanze.* Hamburg: Uranus, 1932.

List, Guido von. *The Secret of the Runes.* trans. S.E. Flowers. Rochester, VT: Destiny, 1988.

Pommer, Josef. *Jodler und Juchzer mit Notendruck.* Vienna: Adolf Robitschek Verlag, 1906.

Reimann Mar-Galittu, Johanna Paula. *Magnetische Aura des kosmischen Menschen.* Trier: Reis, 1922.

Sebottendorf, Rudolf von. *Die geheimen Übungen der turkischen Freimauer.* Freiburg i. Breisgau: Bauer, 1977, 4th ed.

Thorsson, Edred. *Rune Might.* St. Paul, MN: Llewellyn, 1989.

·Key to the Runic Futhork Table

The Rune-rows are to be read from top to bottom. On the right side the sound value of each Rune is provided.

Row:

1 Runic Futhork, 18 Rune row according to G. v. List.

2 Runic Futhork of the Edda according to R. J. Gorsleben.

3 Runic Futhork, the Kylver stone, Sweden.

4 Runic Futhork, the gold bracteate of Vadstena.

5 Runic Futhork Stone from Gotland in Sweden.

6 Runic Futhork, the silver brooch of Charnay.

7 Runic Futhork, the Themes scramsax.

8 Runic Futhork: The holy Row according to Prof. H. Wirth.

9 Runic Futhork of Breza (incomplete).

The other Runic Rows which follow are arranged according to the alphabetic order.

Row:

10 Common Germanic Futhark according to Wilser.

11 Nordic Rune Poem.

12 Old English Rune Poem.

13 Late Nordic Futhark.

14 Futhark of Hrabanus Maurus.

15 Futhark of the brothers Olaus and Johannes Magnus.

16 Younger Nordic Futhark.

17 King Wladamar's Runes.

18 North Etruscan letters according to E. Hubricht.

19 Comprehensive Runic alphabet for those who want to write in Runes or be able to read them.

20 Original Runic numerals from the wheel-cross of the Aryo-Germanic peoples.

21 Runic numerical sequence used by the Armanen.

The last horizontal row of the Runic table portrays the holy whispering Row of Man-Runes. I include a number of Runic Futhorks and Futharks in my Runic table at the back of the book.

44

Runen-Futhorktafel

von Siegfried Adolf Kummer

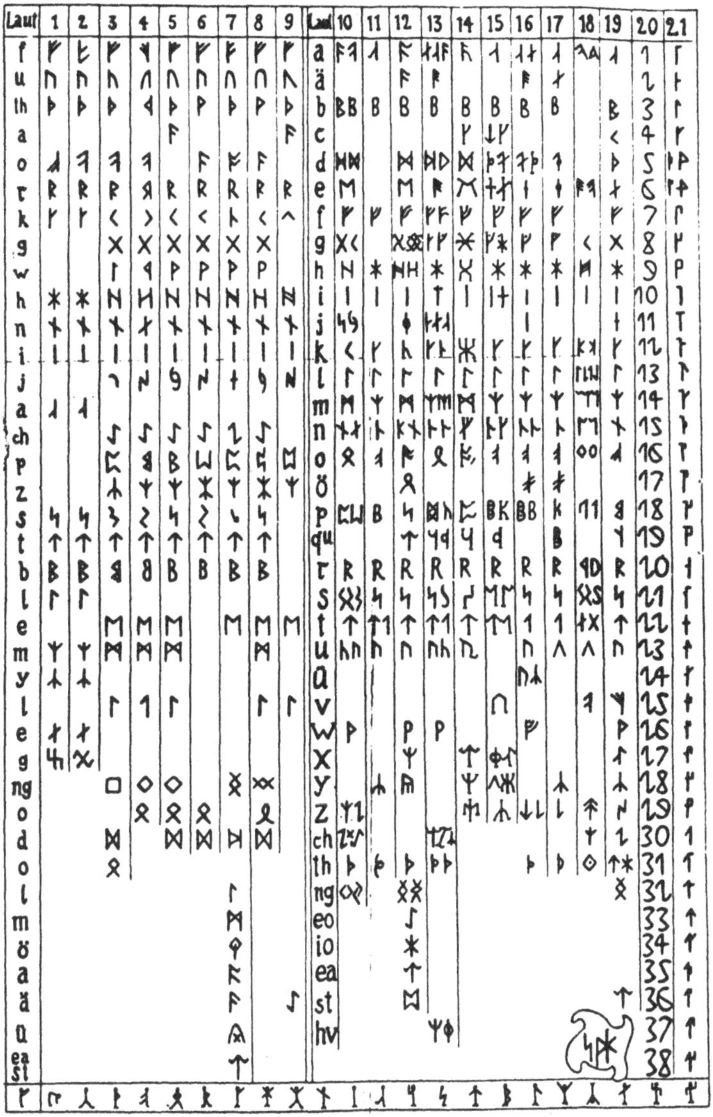
Laut 1 2 3 4 5 6 7 8 9
Laut 10 11 12 13 14 15 16 17 18 19 20 21
f u th a o r k g w h n i j a ch p z s t b l e m y l e g ng o d o l m ö a ä u ea st
a ä b c d e f g h i j k l m n o ö p qu r s t u ü v w x y z ch th ng eo io ea st hv
1 2 3 4 5 6 7 8 9 10 11 12 13 14 15 16 17 18 19 20 21 22 23 24 25 26 27 28 29 30 31 32 33 34 35 36 37 38

www.ingramcontent.com/pod-product-compliance
Lightning Source LLC
Chambersburg PA
CBHW031218090426

42736CB00009B/968